52 TIMES AMERICA WAS AN ASS

The History your Teachers Tried to Hide

This book is supposed to be fun, but on a serious note, the USA really needs to take a long, hard, look at itself and make sure nothing like this ever happens again.

Here are 52 times America was an ass...

1: THE GULF OF TONKIN INCIDENT

While most people are still unaware of it, the Gulf of Tonkin incident was a US-staged false flag operation used by the American Government as the pretext for their invasion of Vietnam. That led to the loss of millions of lives, but the event itself didn't even happen! The US claimed Vietnamese torpedo boats attacked one of its vessels unprovoked. They used this to justify the Vietnam War, but later admitted it was a lie.

2: Torture

The US Military runs secret prisons and camps all over the world where they hide the most "dangerous" of criminals. Guantanamo Bay is the most publicized site, but there are many more. Some of them are even classified as "black sites" and so they are kept secret as a matter of national security. Torture allegations are a common theme in stories from people who make it out alive. The US Military has also been proven to use torture techniques in both Iraq and Afghanistan on many different occasions.

3: Overthrowing Foreign Governments

The US Government and CIA have a long history of backing dictators in foreign countries and funding military coups. The list is long, but some of the countries include Chile, Nicaragua, Cuba, Democratic Republic of Congo, Burkina Faso, Haiti, Iran, Iraq, Afghanistan, Korea, Vietnam, Cambodia, Syria...the list is almost endless. In nearly all cases, the regimes in those countries presented little threat to the United States.

4: Dropping bombs

All countries use bombs during war, but the US is by far the most trigger-happy of them all. During the Vietnam War, the US Military dropped 270,000,000 bombs on the small country of Laos, which officially made it the most bombed country in the world. The thing is, the US didn't even declare war on Laos, and the American public were largely unaware it was happening. The Government didn't help with the clean up effort either, and Laos is still littered with thousands of unexploded US bombs to this day.

5: LYNCHING

The US still has major racism issues, but let's never forget that from around the 1830s, lynching became commonplace in many southern states right up until the Civil Rights Movement of the 1950s and 1960s. Black Afican-Americans who gained their freedom following the Civil War (1861-1865) became the primary targets for lynchings, and experts estimate just under 4000 people lost their life to this terrible and inhumane practice.

6: Eugenics

From the late 19th Century right up until World War Two, eugenics played a considerable role in both the culture and history of the US. Sir Francis Galton led the movement, and many of his ideas would eventually go on to inspire the Nazi Party in Germany in their genocide. Big names involved in the American Eugenics Movement include the Rockefeller Foundation, Kelloggs, the Carnegie Institute and many more. This whole thing helped to cement the institutional racism that still lingers in society today.

7: Native Americans

In the years following the European invasion of America, the Pilgrims went on to massacre millions of people from within the indigenous population of the land mass. Experts estimate that well over 20,000,000 Native Americans died, and that is more than 95% of the entire population. Thanksgiving is somewhat of a farce due to this fact. Everyone might have sat down for a meal together, but the European invaders soon wiped their new Native American friends off the face of the Earth. That is why Native Americans still receive reparations from the US Government to this day.

8: Crack Cocaine

During the 1980s, the US Government allowed Nicaraguan drug cartels to fill LA and other places in the US with cocaine unchallenged. The Reagan administration was caught red-handed letting dealers flood the streets of America with the addictive substance in an effort to help fund capitalist guerillas attempting to overthrow a socialist government in the South American country. Reagan also sold bombs to Iran and funneled that money to his armed friends too!

9: Private Prisons

The US Prison system is almost exclusively privatized. They might have "officially" got rid of the slave trade in the 1800s, but many observers claim they simple rebranded it. The prison system is a for-profit enterprise, and prisoners are often forced to work for little or no pay as part of their sentence. There are currently more than 2,000,000 people in the US prison system (that is more than the entire population of some countries.) An extremely high percentage of them are African-American too. Slave Trade Mark 2? It seems so!

10: STERILIZATION

A study published by the US Accounting Office determined that more than 3,400 Native American women were sterilized without their consent between 1973 and 1976 in the US. Independent studies claim the number is as high as 1 in 4. Some were under the age of 21, and none of them knew they were undergoing the procedure. This was an attempt by the US Government to limit the number of new Native American babies, and thus decrease the amount they will have to pay to them in reparations in the future.

11: MK-ULTRA

MK-ULTRA was a CIA-led mind control program that officially existed from 1953 until 1973, although many people believe it continued much longer. Much of the activities of those involved in MK-ULTRA remain a secret, but it is known that CIA agents regularly gave people mind-altering drugs without their consent, and also engaged in many other illegal activities. The program involved 80 different institutions including hospitals, colleges, universities, and more. What's worse, of the unsuspecting victims whose minds the government was trying to affect, many were not even American. The Government and CIA thought it was fine to run their weird experiments on Canadians too!

12: Slavery

Like it or not, the entire US was built on the backs of black African slaves (there were a few other types of slave too.) Millions of people were taken against their will from African countries and bundled onto boats across the Atlantic Ocean. Many of them died during the journey because conditions were so bad, but those who made it to America faced being sold at a slave market and having their freedom revoked entirely. Slave owners could maim and murder their slaves with no consequences, and they committed some of the worst atrocities in the history of the US.

13: Syphilis

In 1932, the Institute of Alabama ran a program sponsored by the US Government that was supposedly designed to research new ways of curing syphilis in the black population. Many African-American males took part in the study, but the Government failed to tell many of them they had the disease. They also purposely infected many others without their knowledge. A cure was available, but the patients were denied it as the researchers wanted to monitor how the illness progressed. All of the participants were unaware they were being allowed to die for research purposes.

14: Electroconvulsive Therapy

During the MK-ULTRA days, the US Government ran studies in Canada for mind control purposes. Some of them subjected victims to electroconvulsive therapy 2 times each day for 15 days at a time. The "patients" were also put into drug-induced comas for more than ten days at a time while doctors played different audio messages on repeat. It's just one of the hideous experiments called out under the MK-ULTRA umbrella, but one worth remembering. The US Government basically tortured Canadian citizens using some of the worst techniques known to man in an effort to see if they could control their minds.

15: Plutonium Injections

Back in the early 1940s. The US Government began injecting unsuspecting American citizens with radioactive materials. This was called the Manhattan Project for anyone who wants to research further. During the experiments, around 18 people were injected with radioactive plutonium, and more than 800 pregnant females were given tablets that contained high levels of radioactive iron. Alongside this, disabled children were given radioactive breakfast cereal. Sounds like something out of Nazi Germany, right?

16: Mustard Gas

The US Military needed a way to test their mustard gas and the clothing used to protect personnel from the chemical weapon. They chose to expose more than 2500 of their own sailors for the experiment which took place in a gas chamber much like the ones used in the concentration camps of World War Two. Some navy personnel refused to go into the chambers initially, but they were eventually forced to take part by their commanding officers. The information about this incident first surfaced during the 1990s. It is unknown how many people died of their injuries, but experts predict the number was exceptionally high.

17: Recruiting Nazis

Ever heard of Operation Paperclip? No? Then it might be worth taking a few moments to research it online. At the end of World War Two, the Allies had a bit of a problem on their hands. German scientists were some of the best in the world, but the issue was, they were also Nazis. While many of the Allied Powers believed these evil men should go to prison or worse, the US decided it would kidnap many of them, smuggle them to the United States, and force them to work on the construction of the world's first nuclear bomb...which they did. That guy's name wasn't "Oppenheimer" for no reason!

18: Poison in the Alcohol

During the prohibition period of the 1920s when the US Government made the terrible move of banning all alcohol, they ended up killing more than 10,000 American citizens on purpose. In an attempt to prevent the public from drinking alcohol sold by bootleggers, the US Government decided to poison it. That resulted in the deaths of many thousands of people, and was perhaps the worst "preventative" measure ever taken by a government against its own people.

19: Nuclear Bomb

Everyone knows that nuclear bombs are the worst invention human beings have ever created. Many different countries have them, and they have the potential to split the planet in half should a nuclear war ever break out. However, the only country in the history of the world ever to aggressively drop a nuclear bomb on another nation is the US. America dropped two atom bombs on Japan at the end of World War Two, at a time when the Japanese were already beat. Most experts believe the bombs were wholly unnecessary, and they served only as a final US show of strength at the end of the war. At least 140,000 people died in the initial blast at Hiroshima, and many more hundreds of thousands died in the years following. At least 74,000 people died in the initial blast at Nagasaki, with tens of thousands more dying in the years that followed.

20: Philippines

From 1898 until just after 1900, the US engaged in a conquest of the Philippines. Hundreds of thousands of locals were killed, and the military regularly engaged in the murder of civillians. During the conflict, one US soldier wrote to his parents claiming his commander had ordered his battalion to burn an entire village and kill every native in sight. It is estimated that more than 1000 men, women, and children were massacred for no reason at all in this single instance. There were many more.

21: IRAQ

Apart from the fact the Iraq war was totally illegal and it began due to falsified evidence, the US murdered around 100,000 civilians with their bombs during the conflict. They displaced more than 2,000,000 Iraqis, murdered more than 1,000,000, and drastically decreased the quality of life people experience in the country. Sure, they got rid of Saddam Hussein, but at what cost? During the war, US drones targeted schools, water supply systems, and many more civilian sites. No doubt some of the worst crimes of the war are yet to surface.

22: Kurds

The US has a long and confusing relationship with the people of Kurdistan. There are many occasions on which the American Government used Kurds and then left them to die. Take the recent events in Syria, for instance. The US Military did not want to put many boots on the ground in the fight against ISIS. Kurds offered their assistance, and the US used them as the foot soldiers in the war against Islamic State. The American Military provided some funding, supplies, and air support. Tens of thousands of Kurds died in the conflict, so imagine their dismay when the US abandoned them after the defeat of ISIS and left them vulnerable to attack from fascist Turkey. The Turks invaded, many Kurds died, and many continue to die. The US does nothing. Thanks a lot Uncle Sam! Way to look out for your friends!

23: KKK

The fact that the Klu Klux Klan existed in the US in the first place is incredibly distressing. However, what's more traumatizing is that the white supremisist group is still around today with an estimated 1,000,000 members. At its peak, the Klan had more than 4,000,000 members worldwide! Founded in 1865, the KKK is a hate group that primarily targets people of African or African-American origin, and it is responsible for thousands of lynchings and murders of black people. Why doesn't the US Government ban the group and designate it a terrorist organization? Maybe they have sympathies? Who knows?

24: Korea

During the Korean War, 1850-1953, the US backed South Korean capitalists in a conflict against communists stationed in the North of the country. It was an incredibly bloody war with more than 3,000,000 deaths. The US pushed the North Koreans all the way back to their border with China at one point during the conflict, but the Chinese army then sprung into action and pushed the US and South Koreans back to the 38th parallel where it remains to this day. The war never really ended, and the country of Korea still remains ununified today thanks to US involvement.

25: Concentration Camps

Contrary to popular belief, it wasn't the Nazis who invented concentration camps, it was the British. But as it happens, the US loved the idea so much they soon began building camps of their own. Between 1942 and 1945 the US Government imprisoned all Japanese immigrants in concentration camps on American soil. The first of which opened in South Carolina. There were a total of 10 camps, and more than 120,000 Japanese-Americans were incarcerated simply because of who they were. The US has also built and operated many other concentration camps in countries all over the world. Seriously! Look it up!

26: Waco

Okay so everyone knows the guy involved in the Waco incident was a 21-carat nutcase, but that doesn't mean the US security services had the right to do what they did. For those unfamiliar with the incident, a fundamentalist christian psychopath bought a compound, stockpiled guns, and led a group of followers to the ends of their lives. The US Department of Justice could have removed those people from the compound peacefully when they refused to leave, but instead, they used a tank to shoot fire into the building and break down walls, injuring and eventually killing many people, including children. It was a show of force by the authorities, but most folks agree it was overkill.

27: Donald Trump

Electing the racist and bigoted Donald Trump as the President of the US was perhaps the worst and most worrying moment in recent American history. An allegedly freedom-loving nation voted to put children in cages, waste money on building huge walls, and let a madman who believed it okay to "grab a woman by the pussy" run their country. Thankfully, he was removed from office after only one term, so all indications show people are learning from their mistake. Still, letting a man with the IQ of a snail hold his fat finger over the nuclear button has to go down as one of the stupidest decisions a group of people has ever made.

28: Police Violence

There are so many incidents of racist and homophobic police violence from US history that it would be impossible to list them all in a book of this size. Still, let's consider some law-enforcement related deaths of unarmed black people from the last couple of years. American police murdered Vincent "Vinny" M. Belmonte, Patrick Lynn Warren, Andre Maurice Hill, Sincere Pierce, Jonathan Dwayne Price, George Perry Floyd, and many many others. Indeed, there were 1004 shootings of unarmed black people by US police in 2020 alone.

29: Bay of Pigs Invasion

In 1961, the US Government funded Cuban exile combatants who took part in the failed Bay of Pigs Invasion. President John F Kennedy gave permission for the CIA to train hundreds of Cubans in the US, and then ship them to the Bay of Pigs armed to the teeth in an attempt to overthrow Fidel Castro. The Communist dictator and his comrades managed to kill or capture all of the invaders in a matter of hours, and the incident went down as a major embarrassment for the US.

30: Assassinating Fidel Castro

Official CIA records show the organization planned the assasination of Cuban leader Fidel Castro no less than 638 times! The Communist dictator might not have been the best leader in the world, but he had the support of his people, and no-one deserves that many assasination attempts. Actions like this are what led to the isolation of the island and much poverty in the region. Cuban and US relations are still sketchy today, although things are beginning to get better slowly.

31: The Battle of Okinawa

The Battle of Okinawa happened in 1945, and it led to US Military personnel regularly raping women from the local towns for many years. A report from a witness claims the US Marines landed and began looking for Japanese soldiers in the town. As soon as they marked the town as "clear", all the women were rounded up and raped. Local villagers claim three Marines came back to the village for months at least once each week and forced the women to round themselves up and march to the mountains to be raped.

32: Funding the Death Camps

Many different companies from various countries around the world were in some way involved in the Jewish Hollocaust that led to the deaths of over 6,000,000 Jews in Europe. There are plenty of American companies on the list that played a major role in the proceedings. So, for once, this wasn't necessarily the fault of the US Government. It was more the ruthless capitalists in the private sector. Some of the organizations with the worst record include Chase National Bank, Coca-Cola, IBM, and ITT inc.

33: Smallpox Blankets

In 1851 a man by the name of Francis Parkman was the first person to expose a plot by Lord Amherst to murder Native Americans by giving them blankets used by people who had just died from smallpox. He hoped the smallpox-infested blankets would help to eliminate the native population, and they were taken from the dead bodies of soldiers from Fort Pitt in 1763. An epidemic happened as a result of this, and more than 50% of the exposed tribespeople passed away.

34: Operation Big Buzz

In 1955 the US Military engaged in an entomological warfare exercise that involved dropping more than 300,000 mosquitos over Georgia from aircraft. Some "on the ground" dispersal methods were used too. It was an attempt to assess the feasibility of loading mosquitoes that contained yellow fever into planes and using them as weapons in the theater of war. It is not known how many people suffered as a result of the mosquito drops, which eventually happened many times under different names. However, dropping potentially infected bugs over a huge population of your own people is an ass move!

35: Chemical Weapons

You might have wondered where Middle-Eastern dictators like Saddam Hussein got their chemical weapons in the first place. Well, the answer is that in most cases, they were sold to them by the US. During the Iran-Iraq war, Saddam dropped chemical weapons on millions of Iranians and a huge chunk of his own Kurdish population. In one particular instance, this resulted in the death of more than 30,000 people - an entire Kurdish town! All of those weapons came from the US. Smart move! Not.

36: Assassinating JFK

Okay, so, it's true to say that the jury is out on the assassination of JFK. While there are a few feasible theories about what happened, only those involved know for sure. However, one thing is for certain, and that's that the whole thing was planned by either the CIA or forces high up in the American Government. Kennedy had become too big for his boots, and the powers that be decided they'd had about enough. All indications point towards mafia involvement, but the final go-ahead for something like that always comes from the top. A real ass move as he was probably the most level-headed President the country had ever seen.

37: East Timor

Documents released from the National Security Archive prove the US Government approved the invasion of East Timor by Indonesia in 1975. Over the next 25 years, that war led to the deaths of more than 200,000 Timorese folks. Gerald Ford was the President at the time, and records show he had secret meetings with the Indonesian leader immediately prior to the invasion. While the news didn't go public, and American citizens were not aware, the US gave the green light in a bloody and needless conflict that would have been avoided had they opposed the action.

38: Tulsa Race Massacre

In the middle of 1921, mobs of white citizens in Tulsa were given weapons by city leaders and told to kill black people. The massacre happened on two days, May 31st and June 1st, and resulted in the deaths of more than 39 people. 800 were admitted to hospital, and more than 6,000 black residents were interned. The incident happened after a black shoe shiner was accused of assaulting a white woman. It is largely believed the incident never occurred and the whole thing was a result of racist attitudes among the locals.

39: "Winning WW2"

The US Government has long claimed its military "won" World War Two, but the evidence shows that simply isn't the case. 9 out of 10 German soldiers who were wounded or killed during the war were hurt at the hands of Russian soldiers, not Americans. The US has claimed victory since the day the war ended in a real ass move. When you consider more than 26,000,000 Soviets died fighting Hitler, and they were responsible for 9 out of 10 incompassitations, the true story becomes clear. Plus, it was the Soviets who took Berlin, fought through the Reichstag, and raised their flag above the German Parliament. Face it America, you did NOT win the war, and saying you did is farcical.

40: Police Bomb City Street

In 1985, US Police bomb disposal experts were given instructions to bomb a Black Panther house on a city street in Philadelphia. The bomb itself used C4 explosives much like the ones used in earlier years in Vietnam. There were 13 people inside the residence at the time the bomb was dropped from a helicopter, and only two of them got out alive. The rest didn't all die in the blast though. Police actually began firing into the building after the bomb went off, and the ensuing gunfight was responsible for taking their lives. What a nice way to treat your own citizens!

41: Annexation of Hawaii

You might wonder why the Islands of Hawaii are under the control of the United States even though they are mostly populated by indigenous polynesians who settled there thousands of years ago. Well, that's because the Islands used to have a monarchy, but it was overthrown by a group of Western businessmen in 1893, and was then annexed by the US. The United States has formally apologized to the people of Hawaii for their actions in the overthrow of a Government that had mass public support, but it was still an ass move, and not giving the Islands back to the people now is even more of an ass move.

42: The Island of Guam

You might have heard about Guam during the last couple of years due to North Korean missile tests in the area and the media frenzy that always follows. However, most people are blissfully unaware of why the US controls islands so close to Japan and Korea. Well, the truth it all comes down to a war America had with Spain. The US wanted to take the Spanish Philippines, but they realized they needed a base in the area to help achieve their goal. Guam just happened to be in the perfect location. America never had any other use for Guam since then, and refusing to give it back to local people is definitely a major ass move.

43: Collateral Damage

Chelsea Manning spent a long time in US prison for leaking the Collateral Damage video that showed a US helicopter gunship firing on a group of journalists and civilians. Julian Assange who runs the website Wikileaks is responsible for leaking the video alongside the entire Iraq War logs to the press, and he was forced to hide inside the Ecuadorian Embassy in the UK for five years before being taken to prison. The US Government could have held its hands up, admitted it made a tactical error, and begged for forgiveness from the public. However, they chose to pursue the whistleblowers and ruin their lives. It is even possible Assange might receive the death penalty if he is ever extradited to America from the UK.

44: Death Penalty

So this didn't happen on a particular date, but it does happen often in many US states. Although nearly two-thirds of all the countries in the world have now abolished the death penalty in law, the US still wants to retain the right to gas, electricute, and inject people until they die. Some states including Utah also allow death by firing squad! Although they've only killed two "criminals" this way since 1976. Still, for a western country that claims to be the leader of the "free world," it seems a little odd they would want to retain this barbaric practice. That is especially the case when you consider the mounting evidence against its effectiveness. Also, when you know that more than 140 people are released from death row every year after proving their innocence, it's pretty certain the US is executing innocent people regularly.

45: Mexican War

The Mexican-American War happened between 1846 and 1848 following the annexation of Texas by the United States. It was a particularly brutal war that saw whole Mexican towns burned to the ground, and US soldiers raped catholic nuns amongst other war crimes. Over 25,000 Mexicans were murdered by US soldiers, many of them civilians. The US bulked its ranks with Irish immigrants they recruited straight off the boats as they landed. Many of these went on to desert their posts and fight on the Mexican side after seeing all the terrible things the Americans were doing to the catholic Mexicans.

46: The Opioid Epidemic

Since the 1990s, doctors in the US have overprescribed opioid medicines to people who have developed dangerous addictions. Those doctors decided post-2010 to begin refusing scripts which caused many of the addicts they created to turn to deadly street drugs like heroin. The US approach to drugs is one of the worst in the world. All addicts are seen as criminals rather than patients who need help, and there are areas in the country where more than 50% of the population is addicted to one opiate or another. This approach to drugs is largely determined by the US Department for Health and Human Services. Nice one guys! Not!

47: Nukes in Turkey

In most American history lessons, the Cuban Missile Crisis is taught as being the fault of the Soviet Union. US history dictates that the end of the world nearly occured because the Soviets put nuclear bombs in Cuba. However, their placement was in fact in response to the US Military putting nuclear bombs in Turkey. So, in truth, the US is to blame for the Cuban Missile Crisis which occured in 1962 and is documented as being the closest the major powers of the world have been to nuclear war. Definitely an ass move!

48: Ludlow Massacre

During the Colorado Coalfield War in 1914, an anti-strike militia attacked striking coal miners and 21 people including women and children were killed. The militia was made up of the National Guard, and the Colorado Fuel and Iron Company guards. John D Rockefeller was in charge of the company at the time, but he was exonerated and faced no consequences for orchestrating the massacre. The total number of deals during the Coalfield War are estimated at between 69 and 200.

49: Agent Orange

During the Vietnam War, the US Military dropped huge amounts of a herbicide known as Agent Orange on the people of Vietnam. They sprayed more than 20,000,000 U.S. gallons off the stuff all over the country as part of their herbicidal warfare program. The idea was to destroy crops and make it difficult for more crops to grow, thus starving the Vietnamese people. The trouble is, Agent Orange causes some pretty nasty health effects, and more than 3,000,000 people have suffered illness because of it. Some of them still suffer sickness from contamination today.

50: Assassination of Gary Webb

Gary Webb was a little known journalist who gathered evidence and managed to prove the CIA was shipping huge quantities of cocaine into predominantly black neighborhoods within the United States. He should be a national hero, right? Wrong! Gary lost his job, his family, and he was found dead with TWO bullets in his head in 2004. The death was ruled as suicide even though it's pretty difficult to shoot yourself in the head twice. Okay, so, it's possible he might have done it himself, but the CIA ran a campaign against him that ruined his entire life. That's an ass move even if they didn't kill him...which they probably did.

51: Depleted Uranium

Depleted Uranium was used by the US Military during the Iraq War, and it was also recently confirmed to have been used in Syria and a number of other theaters. The US Government claims the Depleted Uranium, which is radioactive, is mostly used in bullets and anti-tank munitions. While the US claimed it uses depleted uranium with low radioactivity levels, the number of people in those areas suffering from cancer and other illnesses linked to radiation poisoning is exceptionally high. Bullets are not enough for the US Military, they use radioactive bullets that contaminate people and land for decades. Ass move right there!

52: Economic Sanctions

From the recent sanctions against countries like Venezuela and Iran, to the long-standing sanctions against countries like Cuba and North Korea, the US uses its financial weight time and time again to bring other nations to their knees. That's a real ass move. If you disagree with the US, it's tough, you'll do as they say. If you don't support the US killing people overseas, tough you'll do as they say. If you just want to be left alone to run your own country and look after your own people, tough, you'll do as they say. Times are changing though, and the tides are turning. The US will do well to remember that all empires fall. It's just a matter of when and how.

Now you've come to the end of this book, don't make the mistake of feeling depressed. Sure, the US has done some of the worst things in the history of mankind, but we're only doomed to repeat them if we forget. That's why it's important we all learn as much as possible about these events and ensure they never happen again.

America is still, more often than not, an ass.

Printed in Great Britain
by Amazon